BOOKWORMS

Community Workers

A Vet's Job

Niles Worthington

Cavendish Square
New York

Published in 2016 by Cavendish Square Publishing, LLC
243 5th Avenue, Suite 136, New York, NY 10016

First Edition

CPSIA Compliance Information: Batch #WS15CSQ

Library of Congress Cataloging-in-Publication Data

Worthington, Niles, author.
A vet's job / Niles Worthington.
pages cm. — (Community workers)
Includes bibliographical references and index.
ISBN 978-1-50260-437-8 (hardcover) ISBN 978-1-50260-436-1 (paperback) ISBN 978-1-50260-438-5 (ebook)
1. Veterinarians—Juvenile literature. 2. Veterinary medicine—Juvenile literature. I. Title. II. Title: Veterinarian's job. III. Series: Community workers (Cavendish Square Publishing LLC)

SF612.W67 2016
636.089092—dc23

2014050274

Editorial Director: David McNamara
Editor: Fletcher Doyle
Copy Editor: Cynthia Roby
Art Director: Jeffrey Talbot
Designer: Alan Sliwinski
Senior Production Manager: Jennifer Ryder-Talbot
Production Editor: Renni Johnson

The photographs in this book are used by permission and through the courtesy of: Africa Studio/shutterstock.com, cover; Robert Daly/Getty Images, 5; Robert Daly/Getty Images, 7; jamesbenet/Getty Images, 9; Sadeugra/Getty Images, 11; wavebreakmedia/shutterstock.com, 13; Goodluz/shutterstock.com, 15; ZSSD/Getty Images, 17; John Daniels/Getty Images, 19; LWA/Larry Williams/Fuse/Getty Images, 21.

Printed in the United States of America

Contents

Who Are Veterinarians? **4**

New Words **22**

Index **23**

About the Author **24**

I am a **veterinarian**.

A veterinarian is a doctor for animals.

You can trust me with
your sick pet.

You can help keep
your pet calm.

A vet is also a dentist
for animals.

I can clean your pet's teeth.

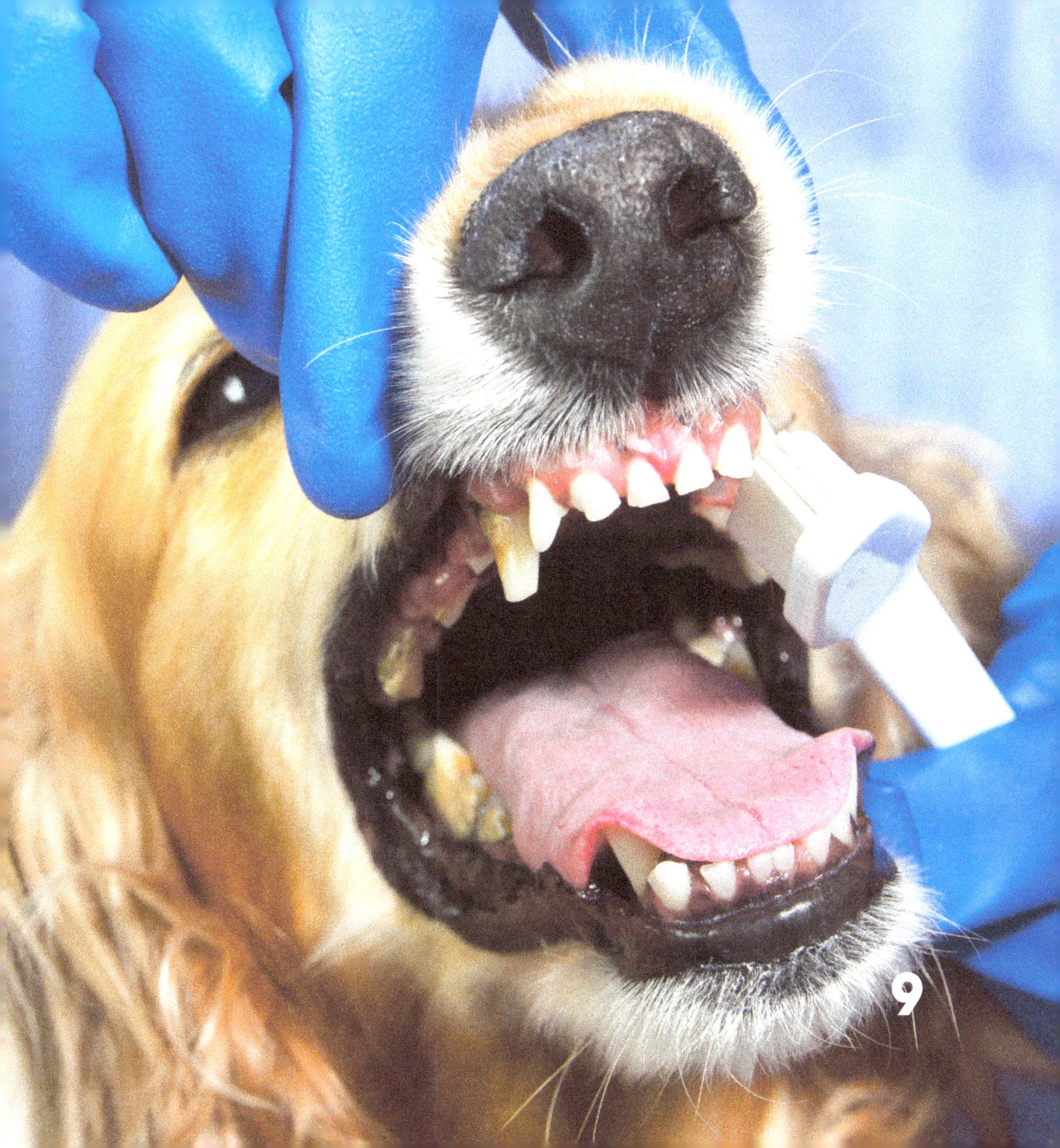

An animal's claws can get too long.

A vet can **trim** them safely.

I take **X-rays** of your pets.

Vets look for broken bones.

Some vets take care of farm animals.

I am making sure this goat is healthy.

Other vets take care of zoo animals.

I am giving this baby panda a **checkup**.

ENRICHMENT
PREGNANCY & NEONATE INFO
和

Sometimes **wild** animals need a vet, too.

This duck hurt its wing.

I like being a veterinarian.

New Words

checkup (CHEK-up) Getting looked at for illness by a medical person.

trim (TRIM) To cut or make shorter.

veterinarian (vet-ur-eh-NAIR-ee-en) A doctor for animals; also known as a vet.

wild (WYLD) To grow up outside of a house or a farm. Raised without human help.

X-rays (EX-rayz) Pictures of bones taken with a special camera.

Index

checkup, 16

trim, 10

veterinarian, 4, 20

wild, 18

X-rays, 12

About the Author

Niles Worthington plays soccer and tennis and enjoys writing children's books. He also works in his family's pharmacy outside of Chicago, Illinois.

About BOOKWORMS

Bookworms help independent readers gain reading confidence through high-frequency words, simple sentences, and strong picture/text support. Each book explores a concept that helps children relate what they read to the world in which they live.